CW00539199

Exclusive Distributors:
MUSIC SALES LIMITED
8/9 Frith Street, London, W1V 5TZ, England
MUSIC SALES CORPORATION
257 Park Avenue South, New York, N.Y. 10010, U.S.A.
MUSIC SALES PTY. LIMITED
120 Rothschild Avenue, Rosebery, NSW 2018, Australia

This book © Copyright 1982 by
Wise Publications
ISBN 0.7119.0101.5
Order No. AM 31428

Designed by Howard Brown
Cover illustration by Tony Meeuwissen

Music Sales complete catalogue lists thousands of titles
and is free from your local music book shop, or direct from
Music Sales Limited. Please send a cheque/postal order
for £1.50 for postage to
Music Sales Limited, 8/9 Frith Street, London W1V 5TZ

Printed and bound in Great Britain by
Page Bros Ltd, Norwich, Norfolk

Songs And Dances Of England

Arranged for

Recorder, Flute & Penny Whistle

Selected and arranged by Liz Thomson

WISE PUBLICATIONS
London/New York/Sydney

ALL AROUND MY HAT

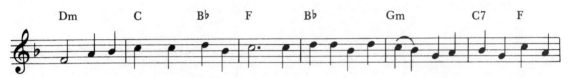

My love she was fair and my love she was kind ___ And cruel the judge and

ju -ry that sen - tenced her a - way For thie-ving was a thing that she ne - ver was in -

clined _ to They sent my love a - cross the sea _ ten thou - sand miles a - way.

CHORUS
All round my hat I will wear the greenie willow
All round my hat for a year and a day
And if anyone should question me the reason for my wearing it
I'll tell them my own true love is ten thousand miles away

2. I bought my love a golden ring to wear upon her finger
A token of our own true love and to remember me
And when she returns again we'll never more be parted
We'll marry and be happy for ever and a day

CHORUS

3. Seven, seven long years my love and I are parted
Seven, seven long years my love is bound to stay
Seven long years I'll love my love and never be false-hearted
And never sigh or sorrow while she's far, far away

CHORUS

4. Some young men there are who are preciously deceitful
A-coaxing of the fair young maids they mean to lead astray
As soon as they deceive them, so cruelly they leave them
I'll love my love for ever though she's far, far away

CHORUS

GEORDIE

As I walked out_____ o - ver Lon - don_____ bridge _____ one mist - y morn - ing ear - ly, _____ I o - ver - heard a fair pret - ty maid _____ was la - ment - ing_____ for her Geor - die. _____

2. Ah, my Geordie will be hanged in a golden chain
    'Tis not the chain of many
   He was born of king's royal breed
   And lost to a virtuous lady.

3. Go bridle me my milk white steed,
    Go bridle me my pony,
    I will ride to London's court
   To plead for the life of Geordie.

4. Ah, my Geordie never stole nor cow nor calf,
   He never hurted any,
   Stole sixteen of the king's royal deer,
   And he sold them in Bohenny.

5. Two pretty babies have I born,
    The third lies in my body,
    I'd freely part with them every one
    If you'd spare the life of Geordie.

6. The judge looked over his left shoulder,
    He said fair maid I'm sorry
   He said fair maid you must be gone,
    For I cannot pardon Geordie.

7. Ah, my Geordie will be hanged in a golden chain,
    'Tis not the chain of many,
   Stole sixteen of the king's royal deer
   And he sold them in Bohenny.

MAGGIE MAY

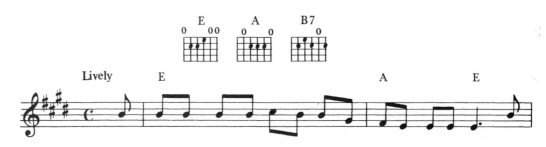

INTRODUCTION: Now ga - ther round, you sai - lor boys, and lis - ten to my plea, And

when you've heard my tale, you'll pi - ty me. For I was a god - damn fool in the

port of Liv - er - pool The first time that I came home from sea.

1. We paid off at the home, from the port of Sie - rra Leone, And

four pounds ten a month was my pay. With a pock-et full of tin I was

ve - ry soon tak-en   in   By   a   girl   with   the   name of Mag - gie   May.

CHORUS:

Oh! Maggie, Maggie May, they have taken her away
And she'll never walk down Lime Street any more,
For she robbed so many sailors and captains of the whalers,
That dirty, robbing no-good Maggie May.

2. Oh, well do I remember when I first met Maggie May,
She was cruising up and down old Canning Place.
She'd a figure so divine like a frigate of the Line,
So me being a sailor, I gave chase.

CHORUS

3. Next morning I awoke, I was flat and stoney broke.
No jacket, trousers, waistcoat could I find
When I asked her where they were, she said; "My very dear sir,
They're down in Kelly's knocker, number nine."

CHORUS

4. To the pawnshop I did go, but no clothes there did I find,
And the policeman came and took that girl away.
The judge, he guilty found her of robbing a homeward-bounder
And paid her passage back to Botany Bay.

CHORUS

THE CHERRY TREE CAROL

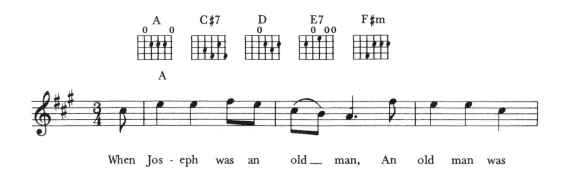

When Jos - eph was an old — man, An old man was

he, He— mar - ried Vir - gin Mar - y, The Queen of Ga - li - lee, He—

mar - ried Vir - gin Mar - y, The Queen of Ga - li - lee. _____

2. Joseph and Mary walked through an orchard green,
   There were berries and cherries as thick as might be seen,
   There were berries and cherries as thick as might be seen.

3. And Mary spoke to Joseph, so meek and so mild,
   "Joseph gather me some cherries, for I am with child,
   Joseph gather me some cherries, for I am with child."

4. And Joseph flew in anger, in anger flew he,
   "Let the father of the baby gather cherries for thee,
   Let the father of the baby gather cherries for thee."

5. Then up spoke baby Jesus from in Mary's womb,
   "Bend down the tallest tree that my mother might have some,
   Bend down the tallest tree that my mother might have some."

6. And bent down the tallest branch 'til it touched Mary's hand,
   Cried she, "Oh, look thou Joseph, I have cherries by command,"
   Cried she, "Oh, look thou Joseph, I have cherries by command."

ENGLISH COUNTRY GARDEN

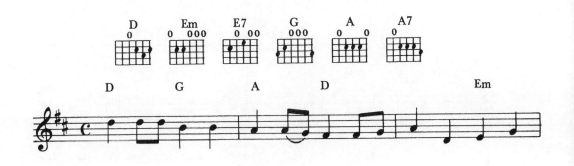

O SOLDIER WON'T YOU MARRY ME?

'O sol-dier, sol-dier, won't you mar-ry me? With your mus-ket, fife, and drum?' 'O no, sweet maid I can-not mar-ry thee, For I have no {coat / hat / gloves / boots} to put on!' Then up she went to her grand-fa-ther's chest, And got him a {coat / hat / pair / pair} of the ve-ry, ve-ry best, She got him a {coat / hat / pair / pair} of the ve-ry, ve-ry best, And the sol-dier put {it / them} on. 'O sol-dier, sol-dier, won't you mar-ry me? With your mus-ket, fife, and drum.' 'O no sweet maid, I can-not mar-ry thee, For I have a wife of my own!'

THE LINCOLNSHIRE POACHER

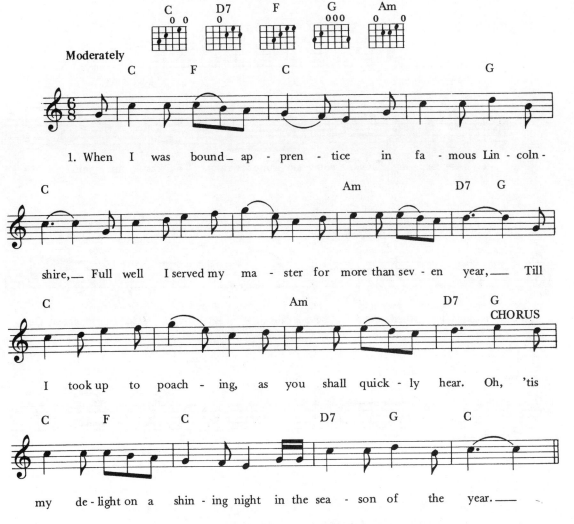

1. When I was bound—ap-pren-tice in fa-mous Lin-coln-shire,— Full well I served my ma-ster for more than sev-en year,— Till I took up to poach-ing, as you shall quick-ly hear. Oh, 'tis my de-light on a shin-ing night in the sea-son of the year.—

2. As me and my companions were setting of a snare,
   'Twas when we spied the gamekeeper, for him we did not care,
   For we can wrestle and fight, my boys, and jump out any where.

CHORUS

3. As me and my companions were setting four or five,
   And taking on 'em up again, we caught a hare alive.
   We took a hare alive, my boys, and through the woods did steer.

CHORUS

4. I threw him on my shoulder and then we trudged home,
   We took him to a neighbour's house and sold him for a crown.
   We sold him for a crown, my boys, but did not tell you where.

CHORUS

5. Success to ev'ry gentleman that lives in Lincolnshire,
   Success to ev'ry poacher that wants to sell a hare,
   Bad luck to ev'ry gamekeeper that will not sell his deer.

CHORUS

GREENSLEEVES

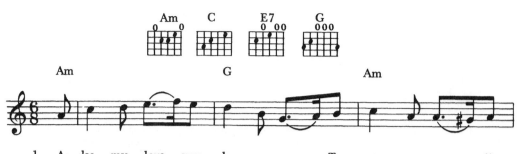

1. A - las, my love,— you do me wrong— To cast me out—— dis -

- cour - teous - ly, When I have lov - ed you so long,— De -

- light - ing in—— your com - pa - ny. Green - sleeves—— was

CHORUS

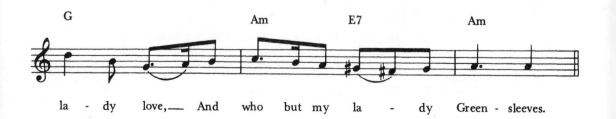

my de - light,—— Green - sleeves was my heart of gold. Green - sleeves was my

la - dy love,— And who but my la - dy Green - sleeves.

2. I have been ready at your hand
   To grant whatever you would crave;
   I have both wagered life and land,
   Your love and good will for to have.

   CHORUS

3. I bought thee kerchiefs to thy head
   That were wrought fine and gallantly;
   I kept thee both at board and bed,
   Which cost my purse well favoredly.

   CHORUS

4. Thy smock of gold so crimson red,
   With pearls bedecked sumptuously.
   The like no other lasses had,
   And yet thou wouldest not love me.

   CHORUS

5. Thy gown was of the grassy green,
   Thy sleeves of satin hanging by;
   Which made thee be our harvest queen,
   And yet thou wouldest not love me.

   CHORUS

6. Thou couldst desire no earthly thing,
   But still thou hadst it readily;
   Thy music still to play and sing,
   And yet thou wouldest not love me.

   CHORUS

7. Well, I will pray to God on high
   That thou my constancy mayst see;
   And that yet once before I die
   Thou wilt vouchsafe to love me.

   CHORUS

8. Greensleeves, now farewell, adieu!
   God I pray to prosper thee;
   For I am still thy lover true -
   Come once again and love me.

   CHORUS

THE LEAVING OF LIVERPOOL

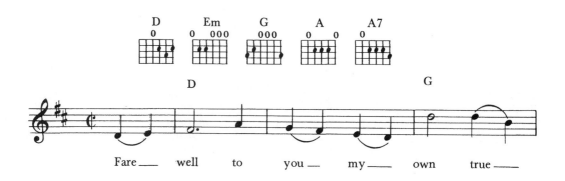

Fare____ well to you____ my____ own true____

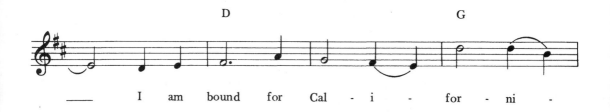

love, I am go - ing far a - way____

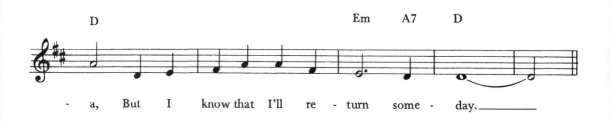

____ I am bound for Cal - i - for - ni -

- a, But I know that I'll re - turn some - day._____

CHORUS:

So____ fare thee well, My____ own true

love, And when I re - turn, U - ni - ted we will be. _____

_____ It's not the leav - ing of Liv - er - pool that grieves ____

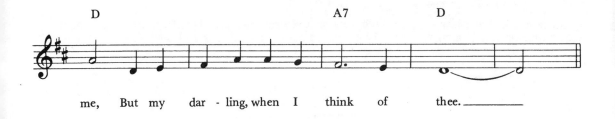

me, But my dar - ling, when I think of thee. _____

2. I have shipped on a yankee sailing ship,
Davy Crockett is her name,
And Burgess is the captain of her
And they say she is a floating hell.

CHORUS

3. Oh the sun is in the harbour love,
And I wish I could remain,
For I know it will be some long time
Before I see you again.

CHORUS

OH DEAR, WHAT CAN THE MATTER BE?

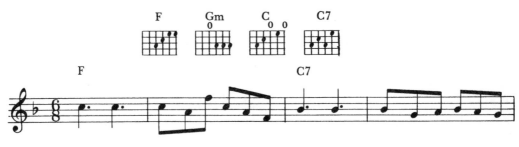

Oh, dear   What can the mat-ter be? Dear, dear! What can the mat-ter be?

Oh, dear!   What can the mat-ter be? John-ny's so long at the   fair

1. He
2. He

prom - ised he'd buy me   a   fair ring should please me, And then for a   kiss, oh, he
prom - ised he'd bring me a   bas-ket of pos-ies, A   gar-land of lil - ies, a

vowed he would tease me; He prom-ised he'd buy me   a   bunch of blue rib-bons, to
gar-land of ros-es,   A   lit - tle straw hat to   set   off the blue rib-bons, that

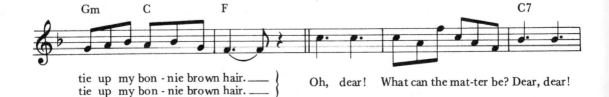

tie up my bon - nie brown hair. —
tie up my bon - nie brown hair. —   Oh, dear! What can the mat-ter be? Dear, dear!

What can the mat-ter be? Oh, dear! What can the mat-ter be? John-ny's so long at the fair.

HOME SWEET HOME

'Mid pleas - ures and pal - a - ces though __ we may roam, Be it ev - er so hum - ble there's no __ place like home. A charm __ from the skies seems to hal - low us __ there, Which seek __ thro' the world, is ne'er met __ with else - where. Home, home __ sweet, sweet home, there's no __ place like home, __ there's no __ place like home!

THE FOGGY FOGGY DEW

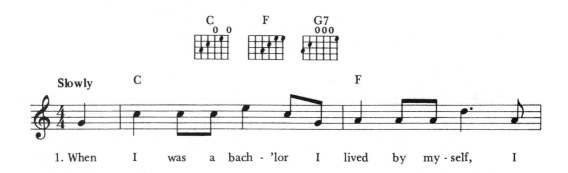

Slowly

1. When I was a bach -'lor I lived by my-self, I worked at the weav-er's trade,—— And the on-ly, on-ly thing I did that was wrong was to woo a fair young maid. I wooed her in the win-ter-time, And in the sum-mer

too, And the on-ly, on-ly, thing I did that was wrong was to

keep   her   from   the   fog - gy,   fog - gy   dew.

2. One night she knelt close by my side
   As I lay fast asleep.
   She threw her arms around my neck,
   And then began to weep.
   She wept, she cried, she tore her hair,
   Ah me, what could I do?
   So all night long I held her in my arms
   Just to keep her from the foggy, foggy dew.

3. Oh, I am a bachelor, I live with my son,
   We work at the weaver's trade.
   And every single time I look into his eyes
   He reminds me of the fair young maid.
   He reminds me of the winter time,
   And of the summer too.
   And the many, many times I held her in my arms
   Just to keep her from the foggy, foggy dew.

DRINK TO ME ONLY WITH THINE EYES

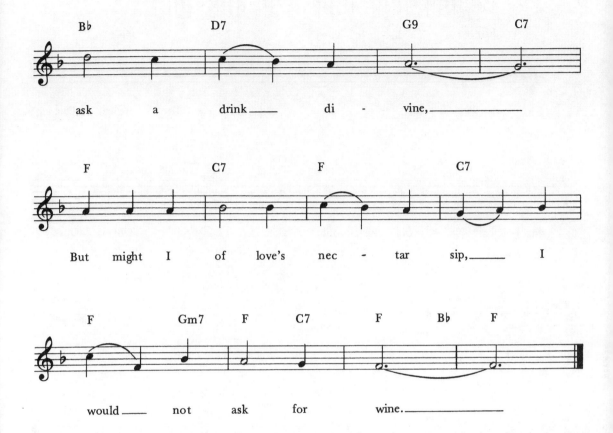

ask   a   drink ____ di - vine, _____

But   might   I   of   love's   nec - tar   sip, ____   I

would ____ not   ask   for   wine. _____

2. I sent thee late a rosy wreath,
   Not so much honouring thee,
   As giving it a hope that there
   It could not withered be.
   But thou thereon didst only breathe,
   And send'st it back to me,
   Since when it grows and smells, I swear,
   Not of itself, but thee.

WASSAIL

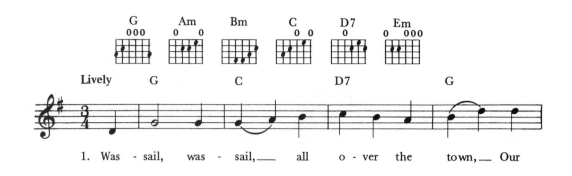

Lively

1. Was - sail, was - sail,— all o - ver the town,— Our

bread it is white and our ale— it — is brown; Our

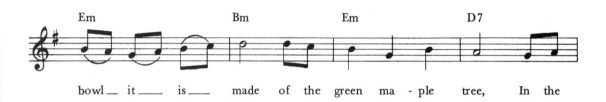

bowl— it — is— made of the green ma - ple tree, In the

was - sail— bowl we'll drink un - to thee.

2. Here's a health to the ox and to his long tail,
   Pray God send our master a good cask of ale;
   A good cask of ale as e'er I did see,
   In the wassail bowl we'll drink unto thee.

3. Come butler come fill us a bowl of the best,
   Then we pray that your soul in heaven may rest;
   But if you do bring us a bowl of the small,
   Then down shall go butler, bowl and all.

4. Then here's to the maid in lily white smock,
   Who tripped to the door and slipped back the lock,
   And slipped back the lock, and pulled back the pin,
   For to let these jolly wassailers walk in.

JOHNNY TODD

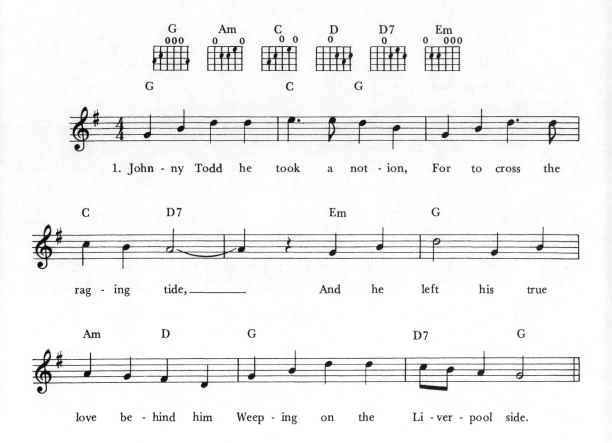

1. John - ny Todd he took a not - ion, For to cross the
rag - ing tide, _____ And he left his true
love be - hind him Weep - ing on the Li - ver - pool side.

2. For a week she wept full sorely,
   Tore her hair and wrung her hands
   Then she met with another sailor
   Walking on the Liverpool sands.

3. "Why fair maid, are you a-weeping
   For your Johnny gone to sea?
   If you will wed with me tomorrow,
   I will kind and constant be."

4. "I will buy you sheets and blankets
   I'll buy you a wedding ring,
   You will have a silver cradle,
   For to rock your babies in."

5. Johnny Todd came home from sailing
   Sailing o'er the ocean wide
   For to find that his fair and false one
   Was another sailor's bride.

6. So all young men who go a-sailing
   For to fight the foreign foe,
   Never leave your love, like Johnny,
   Marry her before you go.

THE GOLDEN VANITY

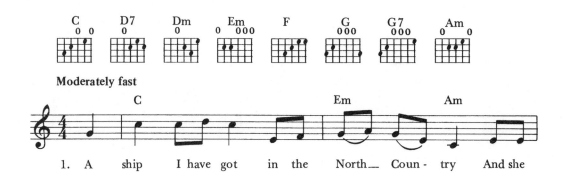

Moderately fast

1. A ship I have got in the North— Coun - try And she

goes — by the name— of the Gold - en Van - i - ty, O I

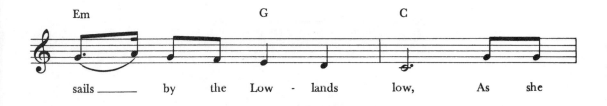

fear she will be tak - en by the Span - ish Ga - la - lie, — As she

sails — by the Low - lands low, As she

sails — by the Low - lands low, by the Low - lands

low,   As she   sails ⎯⎯ by   the Low - lands   low.

2. To the Captain then up spake the little Cabin-boy,
   He said, What is my fee, if the galley I destroy,
   The Spanish Galalie, if no more it shall annoy,
   As we sail by the Lowlands low?

3. Of silver and gold I will give you a store,
   And my pretty little daughter that dwelleth on the shore,
   Of treasure and of fee as well, I'll give to thee galore,
   As we sail by the Lowlands low.

4. Then the boy bared his breast, and straightway leaped in,
   And he held in his hand an augur sharp and thin,
   And he swam until he came to the Spanish Galleon,
   As she lay by the Lowlands low.

5. He bored with the augur, he bored once and twice,
   And some were playing cards, and some were playing dice,
   When the water flowed in, it dazzled their eyes,
   As she sank by the Lowlands low.

6. So the Cabin-boy did swim to the larboard side,
   Saying, Captain! take me in, I am drifting with the tide!
   I will shoot you! I will kill you! the cruel Captain cried,
   You may sink by the Lowlands low.

7. Then the Cabin-boy did swim all the starboard side,
   Saying, Messmates, take me in, I am drifting with the tide!
   Then they laid him on the deck, and he closed his eyes and died,
   As they sailed by the Lowlands low.

8. They sewed his body up, all in an old cow's hide,
   And they cast the gallant Cabin-boy over the ship's side,
   And left him without more ado adrifting with the tide,
   And to sink by the Lowlands low.

BLOW THE MAN DOWN

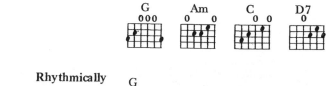

Rhythmically

1. Come — all ye young fel - lows that fol - low the
2. On — board the Black Bal - ler I first served my

sea, With a yeo - ho! We'll blow the man down! And
time, With a yeo - ho! We'll blow the man down! And

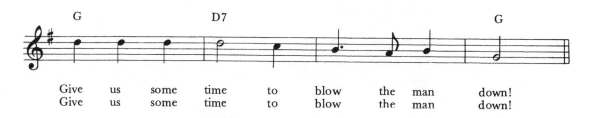

please pay at - ten - tion and lis - ten to me,
in the Black Bal - ler I wast - ed my time,

Give us some time to blow the man down!
Give us some time to blow the man down!

3. There were tinkers and tailors and sailors and all,
   With a yeo-ho! We'll blow the man down!
   That shipped for good seamen on board the Black Ball,
   Give us some time to blow the man down!

4. 'Tis larboard and starboard, you jump to the call,
   With a yeo-ho! We'll blow the man down!
   When Kicking Jack Williams commands the Black Ball.
   Give us some time to blow the man down!

QUEEN OF HEARTS

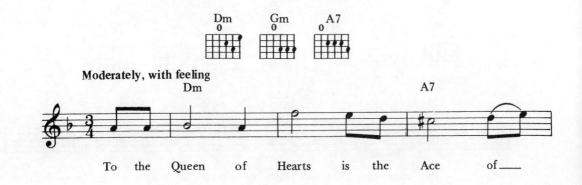

Moderately, with feeling

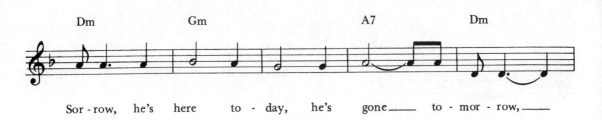

To the Queen of Hearts is the Ace of —

Sor - row, he's here to - day, he's gone — to - mor - row, —

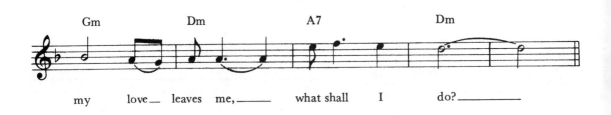

Young men are plen - ty but sweet - hearts — few, If

my love — leaves me, — what shall I do? —

2. Had I the store in yonder mountain,
   Where gold and silver is there for countin'
   I could not count for thought of thee,
   My eyes so full I could not see.

3. I love my father, I love my mother,
   I love my sister, I love my brother,
   I love my friends and relatives, too,
   I'll forsake them all and go with you.

4. To the Queen of Hearts, etc.

THE VICAR OF BRAY

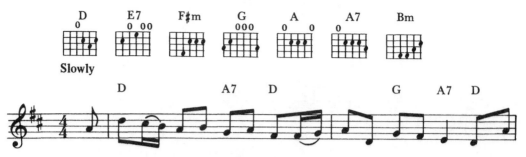

Slowly

In good king Charles-es gold-en time, When— loy - al - ty no harm meant. A

zeal - ous - high church-man was I And— so I gained pre -fer - ment. To

teach my flock I nev - er— missed, Kings are by— God ap - point - ed, and

damned are— those who dare re - sist, Or— touch the Lord's a - noint - ed. And

this is law, that I'll main - tain, Un - til my— dy - ing— day, sir, That

what so ___ ev - er king may reign, Still I'll be the Vi - car of Bray, sir! .

2. When Royal James possessed the crown,
   And popery came in fashion,
   The Renal Laws I hooted down,
   And read the Declaration.
   The Church of Rome I found did fit
   Full well my constitution.
   And I had been a Jesuit,
   But for the Revolution.

3. When William was our King declared,
   To ease the nation's grievance,
   With this new wind about I steered
   And swore to him allegiance.
   Old principles I did revoke,
   Set conscience at a distance,
   Passive obedience was a joke,
   A jest was non-resistance.

4. When Royal Anne became our queen,
   The Church of England's Glory,
   Another face of things was seen,
   And I became a Tory.
   Occasional conformists base,
   I blamed their moderation,
   And thought the Church in danger was
   By such prevarication.

5. When George in pudding time came o'er,
   And moderate men looked big, Sir,
   My principles I changed once more,
   And so became a Whig, sir.
   And thus preferment I procured
   From our new faith's defender,
   And almost every day adjured
   The Pope and the Pretender.

6. The illustrious House of Hanover
   And Protestant succession,
   To these I do allegiance swear,
   While they can keep possession.
   For in my faith and loyalty
   I never more will falter,
   And George my lawful king shall be
   Until the times do alter.

IT WAS A LOVER AND HIS LASS

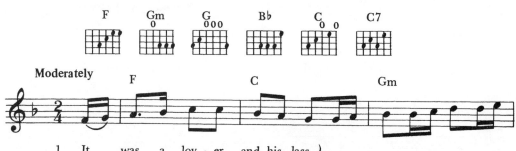

1. It___ was a lov - er and his lass, } With a hey, with a ho, with a
2. This___ car - ol they be - gan that hour,

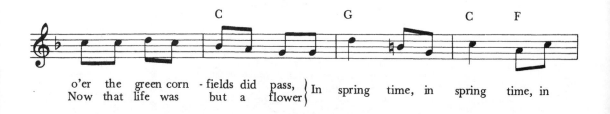

hey, no - ni - no, and a hey_____ no - ni - no, ni - no, {That

o'er the green corn - fields did pass, } In spring time, in spring time, in
Now that life was but a flower

spring time, The on - ly pret - ty ring time, When birds do sing, hey

ding - a - ding - a - ding, hey ding - a - ding - a - ding, hey ding - a - ding - a - ding; Sweet

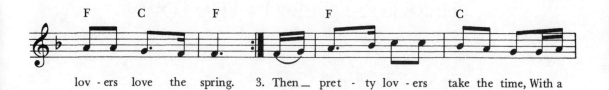

lov - ers love the spring. 3. Then _ pret - ty lov - ers take the time, With a

hey, with a ho, with a hey no - ni - no, and a hey ____ no - ni - no, ni -

no, For love is crown - ed with the prime, In spring time, in

spring time, in spring time, The on - ly pret - ty ring time, When

birds do sing, hey ding - a - ding - a - ding, hey ding - a - ding - a - ding, hey

ding - a - ding - a - ding; Sweet lov - ers love the spring.

THERE IS A TAVERN IN THE TOWN

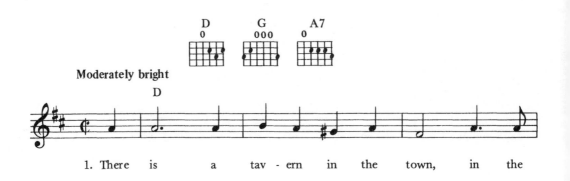

Moderately bright

1. There is a tav - ern in the town, in the

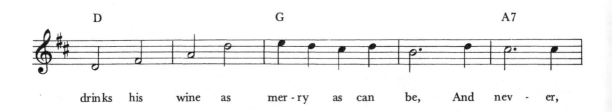

town, And there my true love sits him down, sits him down, and

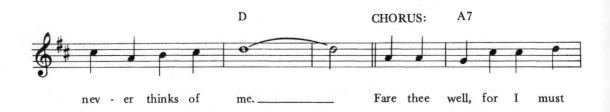

drinks his wine as mer - ry as can be, And nev - er,

nev - er thinks of me. _____ Fare thee well, for I must

leave thee, Do not let this part - ing grieve thee, And re - mem - ber that the

best of friends must part, must part. A - dieu, a - dieu, kind friends a -

- dieu, yes a - dieu, I can no long - er stay with you stay with

you,___ I'll ___ hang my heart on the weep - ing wil - low

tree, And may the world go well with thee._____

2. He left me for a damsel dark, damsel dark.
   Each Friday night they used to spark, used to spark.
   And now my love who once was true to me,
   Takes this dark damsel on his knee.

   CHORUS

3. And now I see him nevermore, nevermore.
   He never knocks upon my door, on my door.
   Oh, woe is me, he pinned a little note,
   And these were all the words he wrote:

   CHORUS

4. Oh, dig my grave both wide and deep, wide and deep.
   Put tombstones at my head and feet, head and feet.
   And on my breast you may carve a turtle dove,
   To signify I died for love.

   CHORUS

THE GAME OF CARDS

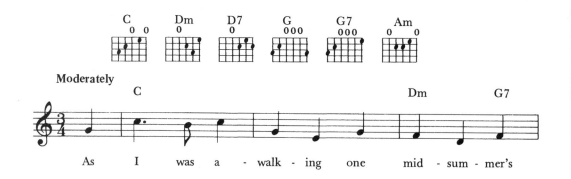

Moderately

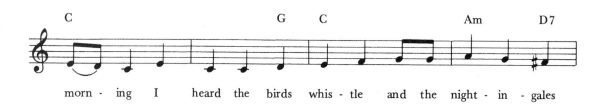

As I was a - walk - ing one mid - sum - mer's

morn - ing I heard the birds whis - tle and the night - in - gales

play And there did I spy a beau - ti - ful

mai - den As___ I was a - walk - ing all on the high - way

CHORUS: C   Am   G

And there did I spy a beau - ti - ful mai - den As___

I was a - walk - ing all on the high - way

2. O where are you going, my fair pretty lady?
O where are you going so early this morn?
She said: I'm going down to visit my neighbours
I'm going down to Leicester, the place I was born

CHORUS

3. It's: May I come with you, my sweet pretty darling?
May I go along in your sweet compan-ie?
Then she turned her head and smiling all at me
Saying: You may come with me, kind sir, if you please

CHORUS

4. We hadn't been walking but a few miles together
Before this young damsel began to show free
She sat herself down, saying: Sit down beside me
And the games we shall play shall be one, two and three

CHORUS

THE BRITISH GRENADIERS

LAVENDER

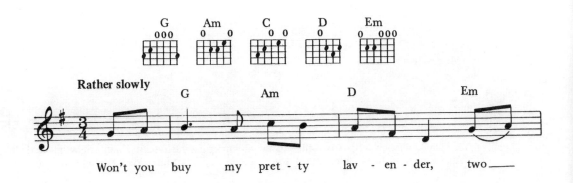

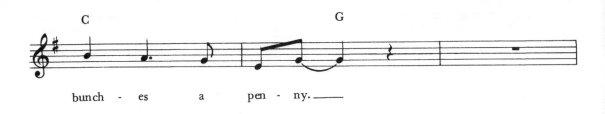

Won't you buy my pret - ty lav - en - der, two ___

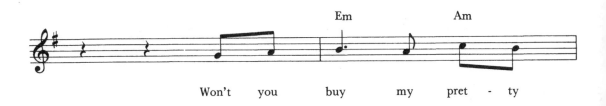

bunch - es a pen - ny. ___

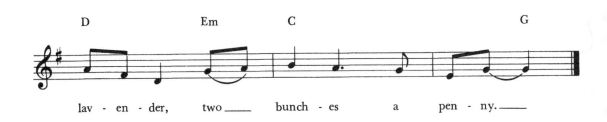

Won't you buy my pret - ty

lav - en - der, two ___ bunch - es a pen - ny. ___

A-ROVING

3. I took her hand within my own, Bless you, young women!
I took her hand within my own, O, mind what I do say!
I took her hand within my own, And said, "I'm bound for my old home."
I'll go no more a roving with you, fair maid

CHORUS

LOVE ME LITTLE, LOVE ME LONG

THE MEETING AT PETERLOO

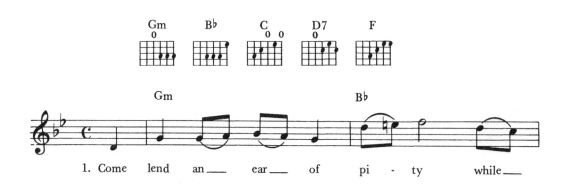

1. Come lend an __ ear __ of pi - ty while __

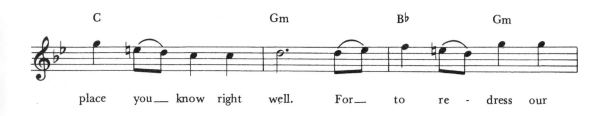

I my tale do tell. It hap-pen-ed __ at Man-ches-ter a

place you __ know right well. For __ to re - dress our

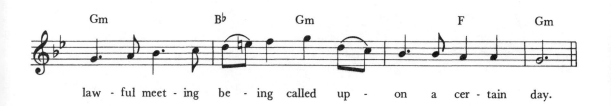

wants and woes re - form-ers took their ways, A

law - ful meet-ing be - ing called up - on a cer-tain day.

2. The sixteenth day of August eighteen hundred and nineteen
   There many thousand people on every road were seen
   From Stockport, Oldham, Ashton and from other places too,
   It was the largest meeting that reformers ever knew.

3. Brave Hunt he was appointed that day to take the chair.
   At one-o'clock he did arrive, our shouts did rend the air.
   Some females fair in white and green close by the hustings stood
   And little did we all expect to see such scenes of blood.

4. Scarcely had Hunt begun to speak: Be firm, he said, My friends.
   But little still did we expect what was to be the end
   For around us all so hard and cruel regardless of our woes
   Our enemies surrounded us on the plains of Peterloo.

5. The soldiers came unto the ground and thousands tumbled down
   And many armless females lay bleeding on the ground.
   No time for flight was gave to us, still every road we fled.
   There were such heaps were trampled down, some wounded and some dead.

6. Brave Hunt was then arrested and several others too.
   They marched us to the New Bailey, believe me it is true
   And numbers there was wounded and many there was slain
   Which makes the friends of those dear souls so loudly to complain.

7. Oh God above look down on those for Thou art just and true
   And those that can no mercy show thy vengeance is their due.
   Now quit this hateful mournful scene, look forward with this hope
   That every murderer in this land may swing upon a rope.

8. But soon reform shall spread around for sand with the tide won't stay.
   May all the filth that's in the land right soon be washed away.
   And may sweet harmony from hence in this our land be found
   May we with plenty all be blessed in all the country round.

LITTLE BROWN JUG

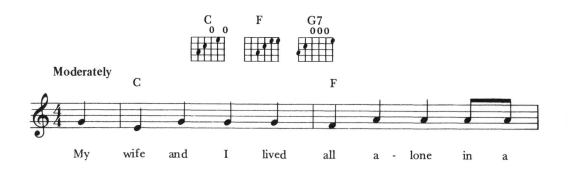

My wife and I lived all a - lone in a lit - tle brown hut we call our own. She loves gin and

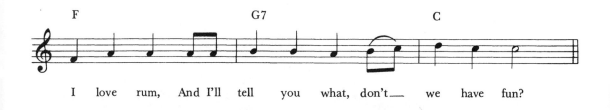

I love rum, And I'll tell you what, don't — we have fun?

CHORUS:

Ha, ha, ha, you and me, lit - tle brown jug, don't I love thee?

Ha, ha, ha, you and me, lit-tle brown jug, don't I love thee?

2. 'Tis you that makes my friends, my foes,
   'Tis you that makes me wear old clothes,
   But here you are so near my nose,
   So tip her up and down she goes.

   CHORUS

3. I lay in the shade of a tree,
   Little brown jug in the shade of me.
   I raised her up and gave a pull,
   Little brown jug was about half full.

   CHORUS

4. When I go toiling on my farm,
   Little brown jug under my arm.
   Set her beneath some shady tree,
   Little brown jug, don't I love thee?

   CHOURUS

5. Crossed the creek on a hollow log,
   Me and the wife and the little brown dog.
   The wife and the dog fell in the bog,
   But I held on to the little brown jug.

   CHORUS

6. One day when I went out to my farm,
   Little brown jug was under my arm,
   Stubbed my toe and down I fell
   Broke that little jug all to hell.

   CHORUS

7. When I die, don't bury me at all,
   Just pickle my bones in alcohol.
   Put a bottle of booze at my head and feet,
   And then I know that I will keep.

   CHORUS

THE WILD ROVER

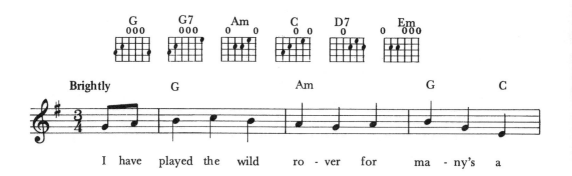

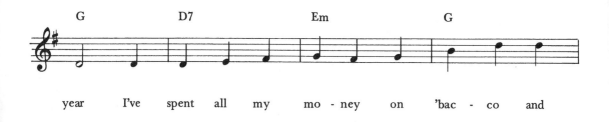

I have played the wild ro - ver for ma - ny's a

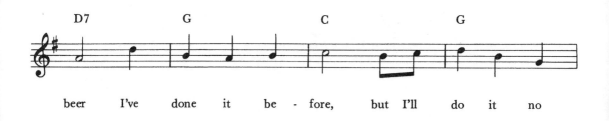

year I've spent all my mo - ney on 'bac - co and

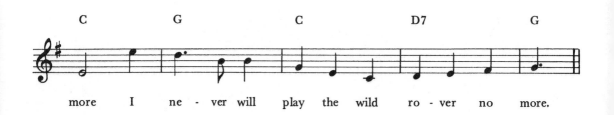

beer I've done it be - fore, but I'll do it no

more I ne - ver will play the wild ro - ver no more.

CHORUS:

Then I'll say: Nay, no, ne-ver, ne-ver, no more___ I

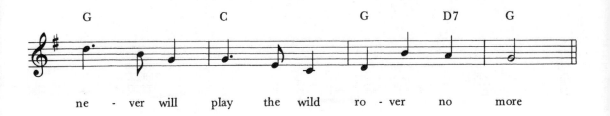

ne-ver will play the wild ro-ver no more

2. I called into an alehouse where I frequently went
   I told the landlady my money I'd spent
   I called for a pot, but she answered me: nay
   We have plenty of custom like yours every day
   And she said...

3. I put me hand in my pocket, so manly and bold
   And up on the counter threw silver and gold
   O stay, sir, O stay, I was only in jest
   I've ale and I've rum and I've brandy the best
   But I said:

4. I'll go home to my parents as I oft ought t'ave done
   And I'll ask them to pardon this prodigal son
   If they will forgive me which they've oft done before
   I never will play the wild rover no more
   Then I'll say...

5. If I'd all the money I'd left in your care
   I would buy a great saddle to ride the grey mare
   I'd save all my money, get it up in great store
   And I'll be a wild rover, wild rover no more
   And I'll say:...

6. So now I'll give over and I'll lead a new life
   And I'll stop all my ramblings and look for a wife
   I'll pay up back reckonings, put my money in store
   And I never will play the wild rover no more
   And so I'll say:...

BLOW THE WIND SOUTHERLY

CHERRY RIPE

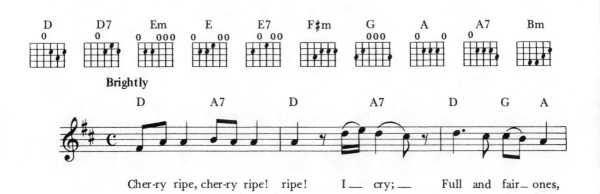

Brightly

Cher-ry ripe, cher-ry ripe! ripe! I — cry; — Full and fair — ones,

Come ____ and ____ buy! ____ Cher - ry ripe, cher - ry ripe,

ripe! I ____ cry; ____ Full and fair __ ones, __ come __ and __ buy!

If so be __ you ask me where __

They do __ grow I an - swer __ there, ____ Where my Ju - lia's

lips do__ smile, There's the land,__ or__ Cher - ry__ Isle,

there's the land,__ or__ Cher - ry Isle. Cher-ry ripe, cher-ry ripe,

ripe! I__ cry;__ Full and fair__ ones, come__ and__ buy!__

Cher - ry ripe, cher-ry ripe, ripe! I__ cry;__ Full and fair__ ones,__

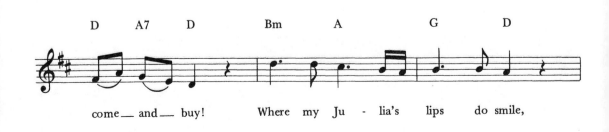

come__ and__ buy! Where my Ju - lia's lips do smile,

There's the_ land, or Cher - ry_ Isle; There plan - ta - tions

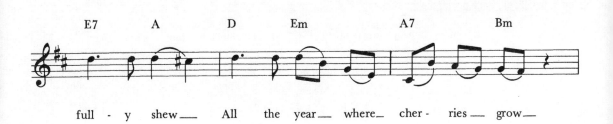

full - y shew_ All the year_ where_ cher - ries_ grow_

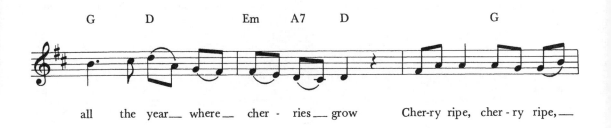

all the year_ where_ cher - ries_ grow Cher-ry ripe, cher - ry ripe, _

ripe! I _ cry; _ Full and fair_ ones,_ come_ and_ buy, _

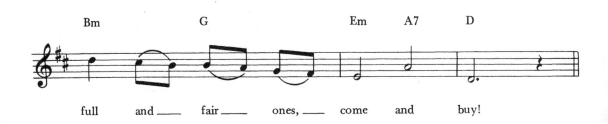

full and _ fair_ ones, _ come and buy!

WIDDECOMBE FAIR

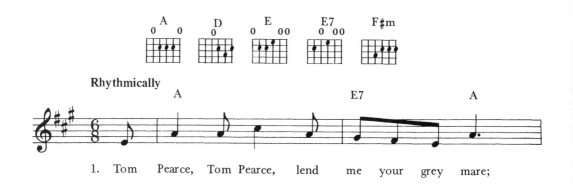

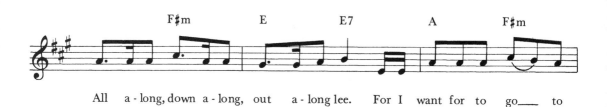

1. Tom Pearce, Tom Pearce, lend me your grey mare;

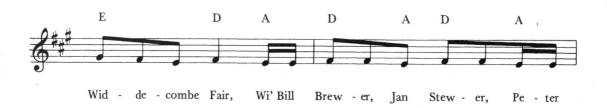

All a-long, down a-long, out a-long lee. For I want for to go___ to

Wid - de - combe Fair, Wi' Bill Brew - er, Jan Stew - er, Pe - ter

Gur - ney, Pe - ter Da - vy, Dan'l Whid-don, Har-ry Hawk, Old Un - cle Tom Cob-leigh and

all, ___ Old Un - cle Tom Cob - leigh and all.

2. And when shall I see again my grey mare?
   All along, down along, out along lee.
   By Friday soon or Saturday noon,
   With Bill Brewer, etc.

3. Then Friday came and Saturday noon,
   All along, down along, out along lee.
   But Tom Pearce's old mare hath not trotted home,
   With Bill Brewer, etc.

4. So Tom Pearce he got to the top of the hill,
   All along, down along, out along lee.
   And he see'd his old mare down a-making her will,
   With Bill Brewer, etc.

5. So Tom Pearce's old mare her took sick and died,
   All along, down along, out along lee.
   And Tom he sat down on a stone and he cried,
   With Bill Brewer, etc.

6. But this isn't the end o' this shocking affair,
   All along, down along, out along lee.
   Nor, tho' they be dead, of the horrid career
   Of Bill Brewer, etc.

7. When the wind whistles cold on the moor of a night
   All along, down along, out along lee.
   Tom Pearce's old mare doth appear ghastly white,
   With Bill Brewer, etc.

8. And all the night long be heard skirling and groans
   All along, down along, out along lee.
   From Tom Pearce's old mare in her rattling bones,
   With Bill Brewer, etc.

THE UNQUIET GRAVE

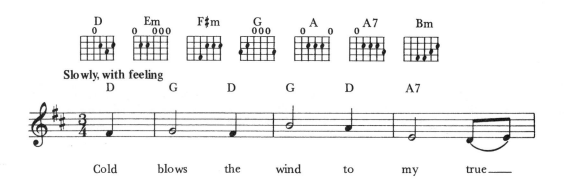

Cold blows the wind to my true love, ____ And gent - ly drops ____ the rain. ____ I've nev - er had ____ but one ____ true love, ____ And in green - wood he ____ lies slain. ____

2. I'll do as much for my true love,
   As any young girl may,
   I'll sit and mourn all on his grave,
   For twelve months and a day.

3. And when twelve months and a day was passed,
   The ghost did rise and speak,
   "Why sittest thou all on my grave
   And will not let me sleep?"

4. "Go fetch me water from the desert,
   And blood from out the stone,
   Go fetch me milk from a fair maid's breast
   That a young man never has known."

5. "My breast it is as cold as clay,
   My breath is earthly strong,
   And if you kiss my cold clay lips
   Your days they won't be long."

6. "How oft on yonder grave, sweetheart,
   Where we were wont to walk,
   The fairest flower that e'er I saw
   Has withered to a stalk."

7. "When will we meet again, sweetheart,
   When will we meet again?"
   "When the Autumn leaves that fall from the trees
   Are green and spring up again."

THE BARLEY MOW

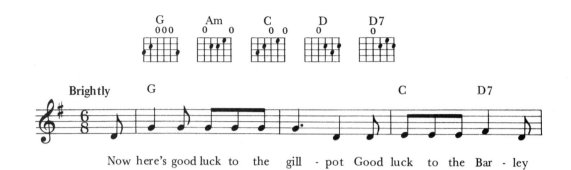

Now here's good luck to the gill - pot Good luck to the Bar - ley

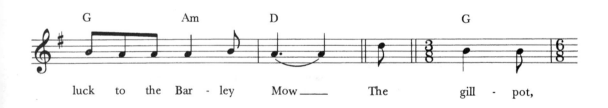

Mow_____ Here's good luck to the gill - pot Good

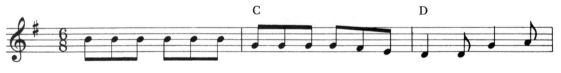

luck to the Bar - ley Mow_____ The gill - pot,

half - a - gill, quar - ter - gill Nip - per - kin and a round bowl. And here's good

luck, good luck Good luck to the Bar - ley Mow_____

2. Now here's good luck to the half-a-pint
   Good luck to the Barley Mow
   Here's good luck to the half-a-pint
   Good luck to the Barley Mow
   The half-a-pint, gill-pot, half-a-gill, quarter-gill
   Nipperkin, and a round bowl
   And here's good luck, good luck
   Good luck to the Barley Mow

3. pint-pot
4. quart-pot
5. half-a-gallon
6. gallon
7. half a barrel
8. barrel
9. landlord
10. landlady
11. daughter
12. slavey
13. brewer
14. company

LAST

And here's good luck to the tavern *(or name of tavern)*
Good luck to the Barley Mow
Here's good luck to the tavern
Good luck to the Barley Mow
The tavern
The company
The brewer
The slavey
The daughter
The landlady
The landlord
The barrel
Half a barrel
The gallon
Half-a-gallon
Quart-pot
Pint-pot
Half-a-pint
Gill-pot
Half-a-gill
Quarter-gill
Nipperkin, and a round bowl
And here's good luck, good luck
Good luck to the Barley Mow

THE LARK IN THE MORN

1. As I _____ was a - walk - ing one
2. The lark _____ in the morn _____ she will

morn - ing in the Spring, I met ___ a young dam - sel, so
rise up from her nest, And mount ___ in the air _____ with the

sweet - ly she did sing; And as we were a
dew all on her breast; And like the pret - ty

walk - ing these words ___ she did say: ___ There's no
plough - boy she will whis - tle and sing, ___ And at

life ___ like a plough - boy's all in the month of May.
night ___ she'll re - turn ___ to her own nest back a - gain.

HEARTS OF OAK

Rhythmically
C

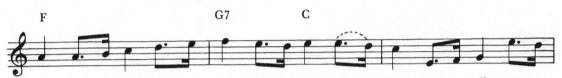

1. Come, cheer up my lads! 'tis to glor - y we steer, To
2. We ne'er see our foes but we wish - 'em to stay, They
3. They swear they'll in - vade us, these ter - ri - ble foes, They

add some - thing more to this won - der - ful year; To__ hon - our we call you, not
nev - er see us but they wish us a - way; If they run, why, we fol - low and
fright - en our wom - en, our chil - dren and beaux; But__ should their flat bot - toms in

press you like slaves, For who are so free as the sons of the waves?
run 'em a - shore, For if they won't fight us, we can - not do more.
dark - ness get o'er, Still Brit - ons they'll find to re - ceive them on shore.

Hearts of Oak are our ships, Hearts of Oak are our men; We al - ways are read - y;

stead - y, boys, stead - y We'll fight__ and we'll con - quer a - gain and a - gain.

57

THE MARGARET AND THE MARY

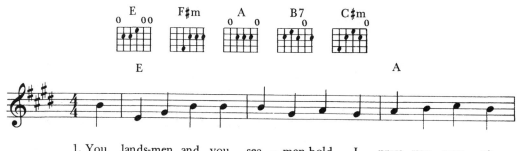

1. You lands-men and you sea-men bold I pray you now at-

-tend. I__ will tell you of a sto-ry on it you__ may de-

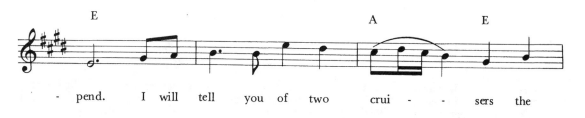

-pend. I will tell you of two crui- -sers the

Margar-et and the Mar- y And__ as__ they were a-

-crui- -sing down in the bay__ of Ker-ry. And__ sing__

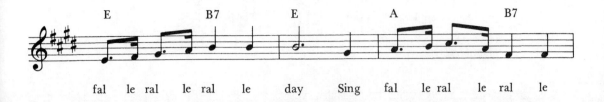

fal le ral le ral le day Sing fal le ral le ral le

Fal le ral le ral le Fal le ral le fal le day.

2. Said the Margaret to the Mary: It's time to make a move
For yonder lies a smuggler all ready for to land
We boldly sailed up to them and unto them did say
Pray are you that bold smuggler that sails from Kerry Bay?
CHORUS

3. Oh yes I'm that bold smuggler that sails from foreign land.
From France unto old Ireland my cargoes for to land.
I'll not show you my papers free nor where I land my cargo
And if you come alongside of me damned little I'll reward you.
CHORUS

4. Then the action it began and it last from ten till one
We beat these saucy cruisers and gave them gun for gun.
'Tis true we beat these cruisers and made them to give o'er.
We've surely sunk the Margaret and the Mary's run on shore.
CHORUS

5. The people of Kerry they all did see the fight.
All on the banks, all on the hillsides stood many a Shannon bright.
'Tis true they all did see the fight, they heard our cannons roar
They've surely sunk the Margaret and the Mary's come on shore.
CHORUS

6. Now landlord fill a bumper and let the toast go round
We will drink to all good people that dwells in Kerry town.
Here's to me and my bold shipmates that never was afraid
Bad luck to all you cruisers, success to the smuggling trade.
CHORUS

HENRY MARTIN

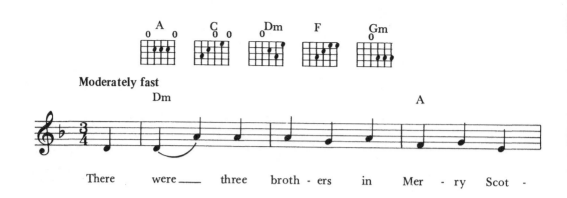

Moderately fast

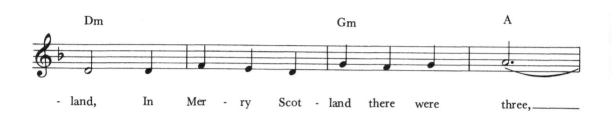

There were three broth-ers in Mer - ry Scot -

- land, In Mer - ry Scot - land there were three,

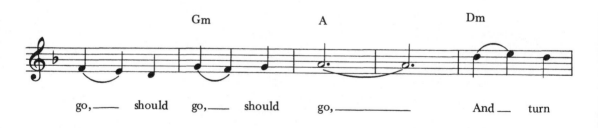

And they did cast lots which of them should

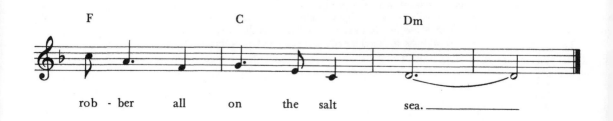

go, should go, should go, And turn

rob - ber all on the salt sea.

2. The lot it fell first upon Henry Martin,
   The youngest of all the three,
   That he should turn robber all on the salt sea, the salt sea, the salt sea,
   For to maintain his two brothers and he.

3. They had not been sailing but a long Winter's night,
   And part of a short Winter's day,
   When he espied a stout lofty ship, lofty ship, lofty ship
   Come a-bibbing down on him straight way.

4. "Hello, hello," cried Henry Martin
   "What makes you sail so nigh?"
   "I'm a rich merchant ship bound for fair London town,
   London town, London town,
   Would you please for to let me pass by?"

5. "Oh, no, oh no," cried Henry Martin,
   "This thing it never could be,
   For I have turned robber all on the salt sea, the salt sea, the salt sea,
   For to maintain my two brothers and me."

6. "Come lower your tops'l and brail up your mizzen,
   Bring your ship under my lee
   Or I will give to you a full cannon ball, cannon ball, cannon ball,
   And all your dear bodies drown in the salt sea."

7. "Oh no, we won't lower our lofty topsail,
   Nor bring our ship under your lee
   And you shan't take from us our rich merchant goods,
   Merchant goods, merchant goods,
   Nor point our bold guns to the sea.

8. And broadside and broadside and at it they went
   For fully two hours or three,
   'Til Henry Martin gave to them the death shot,
   The death shot, the death shot,
   And straight to the bottom went she.

9. Bad news, bad news to old England came,
   Bad news to fair London town,
   There's been a rich vessel and she's cast away,
   Cast away, cast away,
   And all of her merry men drowned.

EARLY ONE MORNING

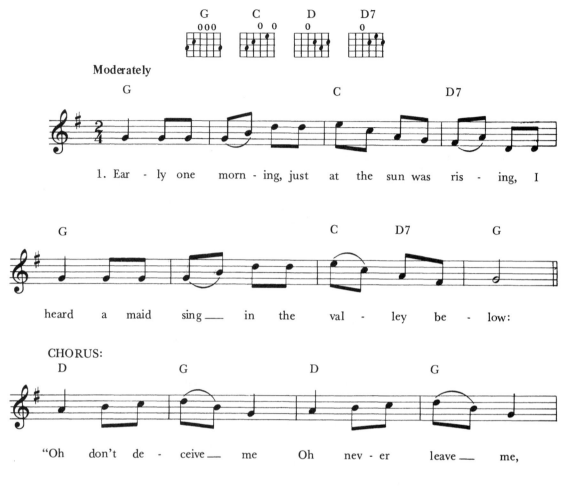

1. Ear - ly one morn - ing, just at the sun was ris - ing, I

heard a maid sing __ in the val - ley be - low:

CHORUS:

"Oh don't de - ceive __ me Oh nev - er leave __ me,

How __ could you use __ a __ poor __ maid - en so?"

2. "Gay is the garland and fresh are the roses
I've culled from the garden to bind on thy brow;

CHORUS:

3. "Remember the vows that you made to your Mary,
Remember the bow'r where you vow'd to be true;

CHORUS:

4. Thus sung the poor maiden, her sorrow bewailing,
Thus sung the poor maid in the valley below:

MATTY GROVES

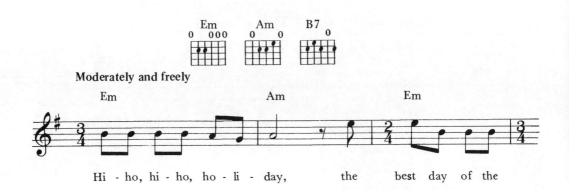

Hi - ho, hi - ho, ho - li - day, the best day of the

year, Lit - tle Mat - ty Groves to church did go some ho - ly words to

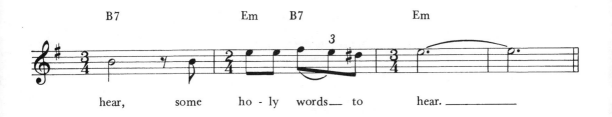

hear, some ho - ly words— to hear.

2. He spied three ladies dressed in black,
   As they came into view,
   Lord Arlen's wife was gaily clad,
   A flower among the few, a flower among the few.

3. She tripped up to Matty Groves,
   Her eyes so low cast down,
   Saying, "Pray, oh, pray come with me stay,
   As you pass through the town, as you pass through the town."

4. "I cannot go, I dare not go,
   I fear 'twould cost my life,
   For I see by the little ring you wear,
   You are Lord Arlen's wife, you're the great Lord Arlen's wife."

5. "This may be false, this may be true,
   I can't deny it all,
   Lord Arlen's gone to consecrate
   King Henry at Whitehall, King Henry at Whitehall."

6. "Oh, pray, oh pray come with me stay,
   I'll hide thee out of sight,
   I'll serve you there beyond compare,
   And sleep with you the night, and sleep with you the night."

7. Her little page did listen well,
   To all that they did say,
   And ere the sun could rise again
   He quickly sped away, he quickly sped away.

8. And he did run the Kings' highway,
   He swam across the tide,
   He ne'er did stop until he came
   To the great Lord Arlen's side, to the great Lord Arlen's side.

9. "What news, what news, my bully boy,
   What news brings you to me,
   My castle burned, my tenants robbed,
   My lady with baby, my lady with baby?"

10. "No harm has come your house and land,"
    The little page did say,
    "But Matty Groves is bedded up
    With your fair lady gay, with your fair lady gay."

11. Lord Arlen called his merry men,
    He bade them with him go,
    He bade them ne'er a word to speak,
    And ne'er a horn to blow, and ne'er a horn to blow.

12. But among Lord Arlen's merry men
    Was one who wished no ill,
    And the bravest lad in all the crew
    Blew his horn so loud and shrill, blew his horn so loud and shrill.

13. "What's this, what's this," cried Matty Groves,
    "What's this that I do hear?
    It must be Lord Arlen's merry men,
    The ones that I do fear, the ones that I do fear."

14. "Lie down, lie down, little Matty Groves,
    And keep my back from cold,
    It's only Lord Arlen's merry men
    A-callin' the sheep to fold, a-callin' the sheep to fold."

15. Little Matty Groves he did lie down,
    He took a nap asleep,
    And when he woke Lord Arlen was
    A-standing at his feet, a-standing at his feet.

16. "How now, how now, my bully boy,
    And how do you like my sheets?
    And how do you like my fair young bride
    Who lies in your arms asleep, who lies in your arms asleep?"

17. "Ah, it's very well I like your bed,
    And it's fine I like your sheets,
    But it's best I like your fair young bride
    Who lies in my arms asleep, who lies in my arms asleep."

18. "Rise up, rise up, little Matty Groves,
    As fast as e'er you can;
    In England it shall ne'er be said
    I slew a sleeping man, I slew a sleeping man."

19. And the firstest stroke little Matty struck,
    He hurt Lord Arlen sore,
    But the nextest stroke Lord Arlen struck,
    Little Matty struck no more, little Matty struck no more.

20. "Rise up, rise up, my gay young bride,
    Draw on your pretty clothes,
    Now tell me do you like me best
    Or like you Matty Groves, or the dying Matty Groves?"

21. She picked up Matty's dying head,
    She kissed from cheek to chin,
    Said, "It's Matty Groves I'd rather have
    Than Arlen and all his kin, than Arlen and all his kin."

22. "Ah, woe is me and woe is thee,
    Why stayed you not your hand?
    For you have killed the fairest lad
    In all of England, in all of England."

JOHN BARLEYCORN

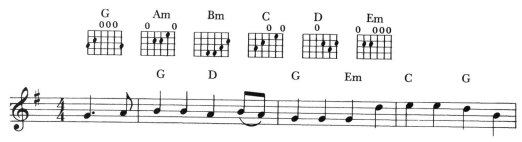

O three men they did come— down from Kent To plough for wheat and

rye   And they made a vow and a   sol - emn— vow John Bar - ley - corn should

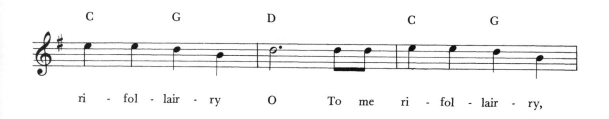

die   To   me   ri - fol - lair - ry, ___   fol - the-did - dle - aye To me

ri - fol - lair - ry   O   To me   ri - fol - lair - ry,

fol - the - did - dle - aye To me   ri - fol - lair - ry ___   O.

2. O they ploughed him in the furrow deep
   Till the clods lay o'er his head
   And these three men were rejoicing then
   John Barleycorn was dead
   CHORUS

3. They left him there for a week or so
   And a shower of rain did fall
   John Barleycorn sprung up again
   And he proved them liars all
   CHORUS

4. Then they hired men with sickles
   To cut him off at the knee
   And the worst of all they served Barleycorn
   They served him barbarous-ly
   CHORUS

5. Then they hired men with pitchforks
   To pitch him onto the load
   And the worst of all they served Barleycorn
   They bound him down with cord
   CHORUS

6. Then they hired men with thrashels
   To beat him high and low
   They came smick-smack on poor Jack's back
   Till the flesh bled every blow
   CHORUS

7. O the next they put him in the maltin' kiln
   Thinking to dry his bones
   And the worst of all they served Barleycorn
   They crushed him between two stones
   CHORUS

8. Then they put him into the mashing-tub
   Thinking to scald his tail
   And the next thing they called Barleycorn
   They called him home-brewed ale
   CHORUS

9. So come put your wine into glasses
   Your cider in tin-cans
   But young Barleycorn in the old brown jug
   For he proves the strongest man
   CHORUS

BLOW AWAY THE MORNING DEW

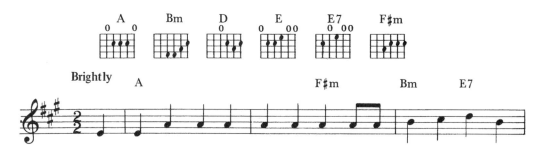

1. Up - on the sweet-est sum - mer time In the mid - dle of the

morn, A pret-ty dam - sel I e - spied, The fair - est ev - er born. And sing

blow a - way the morn - ing dew, The dew and the dew,____

E   F♯m   Bm   A   E7   A

Blow a - way the morn - ing dew, How sweet the winds do blow. ____

2. She gathered up her lovely flowers
   And spent her time in sport,
   As if in pretty Cupid's bowers
   She daily did resort.

   CHORUS

3. The yellow cowslip by the brim,
   The daffodil as well,
   The timid primrose, pale and trim,
   The pretty snow-drop bell.

   CHORUS

4. She's gone with all those flowers sweet
   Of white, of red, of blue,
   And unto me, about my feet,
   Is only left the rue.

   CHORUS

NOTHING AT ALL

2. When I got to the door I looked lumpish and glum,
The knocker I held 'twixt my finger and thumb;
Rap-tap went the rapper, and Kate show'd her chin,
She chuckled and duckled, — I bowed and went in.
Now, I was as bashful as bashful could be,
And Kitty, poor soul, was as bashful as me;
So I bow'd, and she grinned, and I let my hat fall,
And I smiled, scratched my head, and said nothing at all.

3. If bashful was I, no less bashful the maid,
She simpered and blushed, with her apron string played,
Till the old folks, impatient to have the thing done,
Agreed little Kitty and I should be one.
In silence we young folks soon nodded consent;
Hand-in-hand to the church to be married we went,
Where we answered the parson in voices so small,
You scarce could have heard us say nothing at all.

SALLY IN OUR ALLEY

2. Of all the days within the week
   I dearly love but one day,
   And that's the day that comes betwixt
   A Saturday and Monday:
   O, then I'm dressed all in my best
   To walk abroad with Sally;
   She is the darling of my heart,
   And lives in our alley.

3. When Christmas comes about again,
   O, then I shall have money;
   I'll save it up, and box and all
   I'll give unto my honey;
   And when my sev'n long years are out,
   O, then I'll marry Sally,
   And then how happily we'll live!
   But not in our alley.

A Pretty Fair Maid

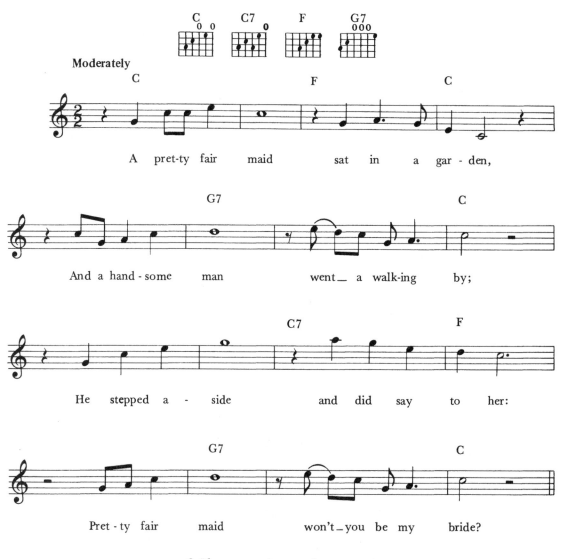

A pret-ty fair maid sat in a gar-den,

And a hand-some man went _ a walk-ing by;

He stepped a - side and did say to her:

Pret-ty fair maid won't _ you be my bride?

2. I have a true love on the ocean,
   Seven long years he's been to sea,
   Though he should stay another seven,
   No man on earth could marry me.

3. Your true love is not in the salt sea,
   Nor is he in that battle slain,
   Nor is he to another married,
   For he is here at your side again.

4. I have six ships all on the ocean,
   And they are loaded to the brim
   If I'm not worthy, of such a lady,
   I care not if they sink or swim.

DANCE TO YOUR DADDY

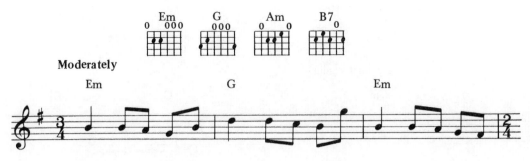

1. Dance to your dad-dy, my lit-tle lad-die, dance to your dad-dy, my__ lit-tle man.

Thou shalt have a fish and thou shalt have a fin, thou shalt have a cod-dlin' when the boat comes in;

thou shalt have a had-dock boiled __ in a pan, dance to your dad-dy, my __ lit-tle man.

2. Dance to your daddy, my little laddie,
Dance to your daddy, my little man.
When thou art a man and come to take a wife,
Thou shalt wed a lass and love her all your life,
She shall be your lass and thou shalt be her man,
Dance to your daddy, my little man.

SCARBOROUGH FAIR

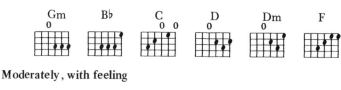

Moderately, with feeling

1. Where are you go - ing? To Scar - bo - rough Fair?
3. Tell her to wash it in yon - der well,
5. Tell her to plough it with one ___ ram's horn,

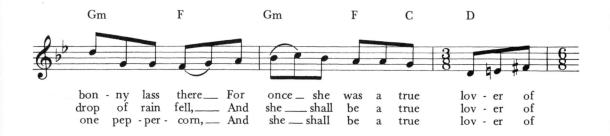

Pars - ley, sage, ___ rose - ma - ry and thyme, Re - mem - ber me to a
Pars - ley, sage, ___ rose - ma - ry and thyme, Where wa - ter ne'er sprung nor a
Pars - ley, sage, ___ rose - ma - ry and thyme, And sow it all o - ver with

bon - ny lass there ___ For once ___ she was a true lov - er of
drop of rain fell, ___ And she ___ shall be a true lov - er of
one pep - per - corn, ___ And she ___ shall be a true lov - er of

mine. 2. Tell her to make me a cam - bric shirt,
mine. 4. Tell her to plough me an a - cre of land,
mine. 6. Tell her to reap it with a sick - le of leath - er,

Pars - ley, sage___ rose - ma - ry and thyme, With out___ a - ny nee - dle or
Pars - ley, sage,___ rose - ma - ry and thyme, Be - tween___ the sea and the
Pars - ley, sage,___ rose - ma - ry and thyme, And tie it all up with a

thread work'd in it, And she___ shall be a true lov - er of mine.
salt sea strand,___ And she___ shall be a true lov - er of mine.
tom - tit's feath-er, And she___ shall be a true lov - er of mine.

7. Tell her to gath - er it all in a sack, Pars - ley, sage,___ rose -

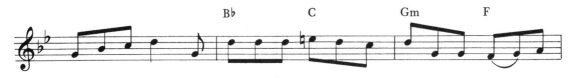

- ma - ry and thyme, And car - ry it home on a but - ter - fly's back,___ And

then she shall be a true lov - er of mine.___

STORMY WINDS DO BLOW

1. One —— Fri - day —— morn when —— we —— set —— sail Not
2. Then —— up starts the cap - t'n of our —— gal - lant ship, A

ver - y far from —— land, We —— there did e - spy a
brave young man was —— he; "I've a wife and child —— in ——

fair —— pret - ty maid With a comb and a glass —— in her
fair —— Bris - tol town But a wid - ow I fear —— she will

hand, her hand, her hand, With a comb and a glass —— in her hand.
be, will be, will be, But a wid - ow I fear —— she will be.

CHORUS:

1. While ⎱ the rag - ing seas —— did —— roar —————— And the
2. For ⎰

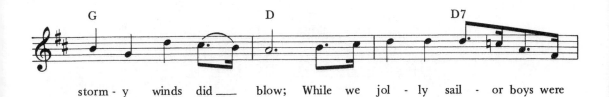

storm - y winds did ___ blow; While we jol - ly sail - or boys were

up un - to the top And the land lub - bers ly - ing down be -

- low, be - low, be - low, And the land lub - bers ly - ing down be - low.

3. Then up starts the mate of our gallant ship,
   And a bold young man was he;
   "Oh, I have a wife in fair Portsmouth town,
   But a widow I fear she will be."

CHORUS

4. Then up starts the cook of our gallant ship,
   And a gruff old soul was he;
   "Oh, I have a wife in Plymouth town,
   But a widow I fear she will be."

CHORUS

5. And then up spoke the little cabin boy,
   And a pretty little boy was he;
   "Oh, I am more grieved for my daddy and my mammy,
   Than you for your wives all three."

CHORUS

6. Then three times round went our gallant ship,
   And three times round went she;
   For the want of a life-boat, they all went down,
   And she sank to the bottom of the sea.

CHORUS

ILKLEY MOOR BAHT'AT

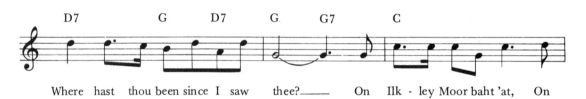

2. I've been a-courting Mary Jane,
   On Ilkley Moor baht 'at.
   I've been a-courting Mary Jane,
   I've been a-courting Mary Jane.

   CHORUS

3. Thou'll surely catch thy death of cold. . .

4. Then we shall have to bury thee. . .

5. Then worms will come and et thee oop. . .

6. Then dooks will come and et oop worms. . .

7. Then we will come and et oop dooks. . .

8. Then we will have thee back again. . .